ROMAN LIFE

BY

JOHN GUY

Who were the Ancient Romans?

The emergence of ancient Rome as a power in the Mediterranean was a long, slow process and owed much to the Greek civilization that preceded it. The lands around the Mediterranean were not unified under a central political system, but consisted of a number of independent city-states; self-governing regions comprising a large town, several villages and the lands between. By tradition, the small city-state of Rome was said to be created in 753 BC. Its inhabitants were a mixture of Etruscans (who ruled over much of Italy) and Latins (from southern Italy). They collectively became known as Romans. From about 550 BC Rome was ruled by Etruscan kings, but in 509 BC the Romans drove the king out and Rome became a tiny, independent republic.

HIGH STANDARD OF LIVING

With the expansion of the Roman Empire came great wealth. Riches were brought from abroad, along with slaves to do the menial tasks. This meant that the average Roman lived comfortably, with a minority living extremely well.

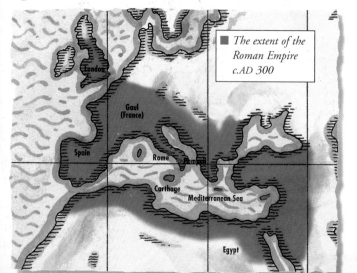

■ *The extent of the Roman Empire c.AD 300*

London

Gaul (France)

Spain

Rome

Pompeii

Carthage

Mediterranean Sea

Egypt

A NIGHT ON THE TOWN

The Romans learnt much from Greek architecture but went on to develop their own style. They perfected the semi-circular arch which allowed them to build higher, more magnificent structures, many of which are still standing today. Most Roman towns had huge amphitheatres for the entertainment of the masses, where they staged plays, sporting events and even blood sports.

THE MIGHT OF ROME

The strength and growth of the Roman Empire lay with its military efficiency. The Romans were able to organise a centrally controlled army, something no other civilisation had managed. Divided into legions of about 5,000 men, the army was well equipped and very disciplined compared with its adversaries who still fought in small, disorganised bands. Few armies could resist the might of the Roman legions.

ROMULUS & REMUS

According to legend, the state of Rome was founded by the twin brothers Romulus and Remus. They were said to be descendants of the Roman god Mars and Rhea Silvia, daughter of Numitor, king of Alba Lenga. The twins were thrown into the Tiber River by a wicked great uncle, hoping they would drown. Fortunately they were washed ashore and were saved by a she-wolf (as depicted here). A shepherd brought them up and later they were reunited with their grandfather, King Numitor. As adults, they quarrelled over who should rule Rome, the city they had both founded. Romulus killed Remus in 753 BC to become king. The clan of Romulus were Latins, from Latium, a district south and west of the Tiber River and its valley.

STRUCTURED SOCIETY

Roman society was very structured. Young men were encouraged to learn a trade or join the army; women to create a stable family background. Although people were mostly illiterate, writing was encouraged in wealthy and political circles to record the greatness of the Empire. Latin, the basis for many modern languages, became the language of the Romans as the Etruscan language died out.

HEARTH & HOME

The typical house of a wealthy Roman contained an impressive entrance vestibule, called an atrium, which was often open to the sky and may have had a fountain or pool as a central feature. It would also include a *lararium*, as shown here, which was a household shrine to worship domestic gods and godesses, such as the goddess of the hearth, Vesta.

LITERACY

Many nobles could read and write having been educated by private tutors as children. The girl shown above is using a stylus to inscribe a wax tablet. Romans also wrote with metal nibbed or hollow reed pens on papyrus paper or vellum (stretched animal skin).

HOME COMFORTS

Many of the richest Roman citizens had two houses, a town house and a country villa. Furnishings were kept simple and decoration was plain, yet elegant. Larger Roman houses had few windows, to keep out the heat of the sun, and usually had at least one open courtyard, complete with fountain. Floors and walls were kept cool with the prodigious use of marble or stone tiles, often inlaid with elaborate mosaics, as shown here.

TAKING IT EASY

This elegant couch was used to recline on for an afternoon nap. It would also have been used at mealtimes to seat two or three guests. Food would have been placed on low tables with several such seats arranged around them.

Life for the Rich

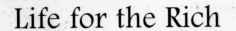

A great many of the things we usually associate with the Romans, such as their luxurious lifestyle, are better associated with the rich than with Romans in general. As in most societies of the past, the artefacts which have survived the passage of time are not necessarily those which best represent that society. The items shown on these pages would have been known to a comparative few: the rich and elite of society. The high standard and sheer quality are a testament to the heights of sophistication reached by Roman civilization. In many cases such standards of living were not achieved again until the late 19th century.

The larger houses had their own plumbed water supply and many were also furnished with a hypocaust – under-floor central heating.

A STABLE SOCIETY

The Roman Empire, for a time at least, brought peace and stability to central and southern Europe (a period known as the Roman Peace), and with it came prosperity, certainly for the ruling classes. Roman coinage was distributed throughout the empire to provide a common monetary unit and make trade between the member nations easier.

SOCIAL STANDING

Roman society made great use of slavery. Unfortunate prisoners captured from conquered lands were put to work as menial labourers or were employed as servants in wealthy households. Society was divided into tiers, comprising citizens; non-citizens (or provincials), who had fewer rights; and slaves, who had no rights at all.

THE FORUM

The central meeting place in a typical Roman town was called the forum, from the Latin word *foris*, which means 'outside'. It began as a simple open space where weekly markets were held. Forums evolved into important centres of commerce, where the wealthy conducted their business.

Life for the Poor

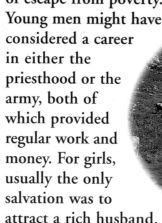

The Roman world was full of contradictions and paradoxes. Its culture was one of the most sophisticated; its society one of the richest ever known, providing untold wealth and splendour for some. However, for most people life was oppressive. The increasing cost of maintaining the Empire placed an excessive tax demand on all classes. The poor strongly resented the leisurely and flamboyant lifestyles of the rich. There was no infrastructure of social care in Roman society; the poor were largely left to fend for themselves as best they could. There were few means of escape from poverty. Young men might have considered a career in either the priesthood or the army, both of which provided regular work and money. For girls, usually the only salvation was to attract a rich husband.

CREATURE COMFORTS

The poor had few comforts or luxuries. Housing conditions were usually squalid, with no sanitation. There were public baths, but they were not free and rarely could the very poor afford them. Town dwellers often had to use public toilet facilities. Water was at least clean and free, collected from public fountains. Lighting was normally by oil lamps (shown above) burning olive oil.

LIFE IN THE TOWNS

In the towns most poor people lived in cramped, low-quality tenement housing. Several stories of apartments were built over open-fronted shops or workshops. Few people in towns provided their own food, they bought their supplies from country people who took any excess they had to market. Townspeople usually earned their living providing a service or trade, working in shops, or as clerks for the Roman civil service. The picture shows the remains of a typical town street in Pompeii, in south-west Italy.

LIFE IN THE COUNTRY

Most country dwellers were poor, eking out a subsistence living on small family farms. Cows were kept for their milk (to drink and to make into cheese). Poultry was kept for eggs. Meat was only occasionally served at table. All members of the family were expected to work, including the children. The men looked after the livestock and carried out heavy tasks, such as ploughing. Women tended the crops, looked after the house and family, and made clothes. The children would help with domestic chores and wherever they could around the farm.

SUBSISTENCE FARMING

By today's standards, Roman farming methods were quite primitive and inefficient, though by the standards of their day Roman agriculture was superior to most other Mediterranean countries. The Romans invented a new form of plough, using a strong metal blade to replace its wood or bone predecessor. It was able to cut a deeper furrow, very important when farming in the poor infertile soils of hot countries. Sugar was unknown in the Roman world so bees were kept to manufacture honey as a sweetener.

FAMILY LIFE

Family life was very important to the Romans, whether rich or poor. There were no pensions so the responsibility for looking after elderly relatives fell on the entire family. Most people continued working until they were either too frail, or died.

Food & Drink

By all accounts Romans from all classes ate and drank comparatively well. Their diet was probably very similar to that still enjoyed in many parts of the Mediterranean today, consisting of plenty of fresh fruit and vegetables, supplemented by fish and poultry. Red meat was seldom eaten in Roman society. Salads were common at mealtimes and were often used as a garnish, since the look of a dish was just as important to Romans as its taste. Even the poor were better nourished than their contemporaries in other regions of the known world. Their staple diet was bread and vegetables and their main meal would have taken place after the day's work. For the rich, mealtimes were an excuse for social gatherings, starting in the middle of the afternoon and continuing over several hours. Cooking utensils and pots were usually made of bronze for the wealthy, or earthenware for the poor. They ate with knives only, so finger bowls were provided to keep hands clean.

THE SPICE OF LIFE

Roman housewives would be familiar with many of the herbs used by modern cooks to add flavour and interest to their meals, such as parsley, thyme, fennel, fenugreek, angelica and mint. Spices, imported from the East, were used to disguise the often rancid taste of food, particularly meat, that might not keep well in the Mediterranean heat.

SERVING VESSELS

Romans used a variety of vessels both to serve and drink wine. Jugs and wine cups were made out of pottery, bronze or glass (as shown here), or even finely engraved silver.

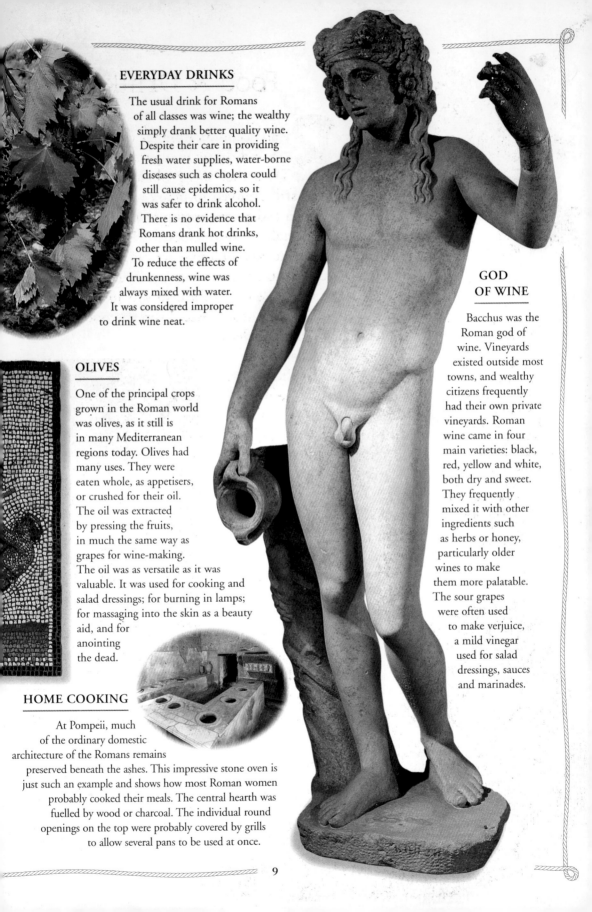

EVERYDAY DRINKS

The usual drink for Romans of all classes was wine; the wealthy simply drank better quality wine. Despite their care in providing fresh water supplies, water-borne diseases such as cholera could still cause epidemics, so it was safer to drink alcohol. There is no evidence that Romans drank hot drinks, other than mulled wine. To reduce the effects of drunkenness, wine was always mixed with water. It was considered improper to drink wine neat.

OLIVES

One of the principal crops grown in the Roman world was olives, as it still is in many Mediterranean regions today. Olives had many uses. They were eaten whole, as appetisers, or crushed for their oil. The oil was extracted by pressing the fruits, in much the same way as grapes for wine-making. The oil was as versatile as it was valuable. It was used for cooking and salad dressings; for burning in lamps; for massaging into the skin as a beauty aid, and for anointing the dead.

HOME COOKING

At Pompeii, much of the ordinary domestic architecture of the Romans remains preserved beneath the ashes. This impressive stone oven is just such an example and shows how most Roman women probably cooked their meals. The central hearth was fuelled by wood or charcoal. The individual round openings on the top were probably covered by grills to allow several pans to be used at once.

GOD OF WINE

Bacchus was the Roman god of wine. Vineyards existed outside most towns, and wealthy citizens frequently had their own private vineyards. Roman wine came in four main varieties: black, red, yellow and white, both dry and sweet. They frequently mixed it with other ingredients such as herbs or honey, particularly older wines to make them more palatable. The sour grapes were often used to make verjuice, a mild vinegar used for salad dressings, sauces and marinades.

9

THEATRICS

Romans were great theatregoers. Most towns had an amphitheatre, usually open to the sky, so most performances took place during the day. Only men could become actors (women's roles were played by boys) and each character wore a mask to represent their character.

BLOOD SPORTS

Romans loved to watch blood sports. The entertainment at arenas was usually organized by the emperor or other dignitaries to win popularity. They usually went on all day. First, wild animals such as lions and tigers were brought in to kill one another (at the inauguration of the Colosseum, 5,000 wild animals were slaughtered in a single day). This progressed to pitting defenceless slaves or religious martyrs against the animals. Condemned criminals had to fight one another and contests usually went on to the death.

CHARIOT RACING

Most of the larger Roman towns had a stadium (an elongated arena) where chariot races were staged. Small, two-wheeled carts were pulled by two to four horses at great speed around a track. The excitement was intense as the public bet on the outcome. Accidents were common, frequently resulting in death.

THE COLOSSEUM

The Colosseum in Rome was the greatest amphitheatre ever built. Unlike other theatres it seems not to have been designed for the performances of plays, but for spectator sports to amuse the crowds. It was built to a brilliant design and was free standing (most amphitheatres were built into a natural depression in a hillside), and it could seat 50,000 people. Its specially constructed floor could be filled with water to allow the enactment of sea battles.

Pastimes

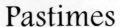

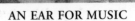

Even average Romans, who spent most of their time working for a living, considered entertainment an essential part of life. They regularly enjoyed going to the theatre, or to the arena to watch sporting events. The Romans had many gods to worship so there was almost always a feast day to celebrate, many of which became a good excuse for a festival of music and dance. Rich nobles preferred to hire musicians to play at their private banquets rather than join in large public displays. The wealthy also spent a great deal of time going to the baths, where they met friends, exchanged gossip, and enjoyed the waters.

AN EAR FOR MUSIC

Music accompanied most religious ceremonies or events at the arena, though dancing was usually reserved for the poorer classes. Instruments were quite simple, such as flutes, pan pipes and lyres (shown here being played by Apollo, the Roman god of light, poetry and music).

GLADIATORS

The most spectacular event at the Colosseum was watching the gladiators fight to the death. Gladiators were usually criminals or slaves and were trained to fight in special schools. Occasionally, women were trained to become gladiators.

Fashion

FOOT LOOSE

Both men and women favoured open sandals, for ventilation in the hot sun. They came in various styles, but were usually flat, or with very low heels. The thongs and straps were made of leather. The soles were usually made of shaped wood (or heavy hide), sometimes with studs for longer wear.

*T*he Roman Empire spanned nearly 700 years (though there were periods of ascendancy and decline) which meant that fashions changed quite considerably, though the change was probably gradual from generation to generation. Children did not have their own fashions, as now, but wore clothes that were miniature copies of adult clothes. Because of the hot climate, the emphasis was on keeping cool. Generally, light materials were used, which might have included silks from China or cotton from India, for those who could afford these expensive imports. Both men and women were quite fastidious about their appearance. In general, light colours (often white) were preferred. The colour purple, still associated with royalty, was first adopted by the Romans as a symbol of power. It was the most expensive clothes dye to produce. Officials wore togas with a purple stripe, but only the emperor could wear a totally purple toga.

MIRROR, MIRROR

Because the technique of manufacturing mirror glass had not yet been perfected, the Romans made mirrors by highly polishing pieces of metal, usually silver or bronze. This beautiful example was finely engraved on the reverse side.

CHANGING FACE OF FASHION

Roman women favoured coiffured hairstyles, pinned back and held in place with a comb. It was fashionable for women to keep a pale complexion, difficult in the Mediterranean sun. Many women covered their faces as much as possible, while others applied chalk dust as a face powder.

LOOKING GOOD

Women of all classes wore jewellery. Those who could afford it wore gold and silver necklaces, bracelets and earrings, decorated with jewels or rare stones. Bronze was used as a cheaper substitute, embellished with coloured glass beads to resemble jewels, rather in the manner of costume jewellery today. Both men and women wore rings. Perfumes were widely available, mostly made from plant extracts.

THE TOGA

The toga was the national dress of Rome and it was the right of all free-born citizens to wear it. But contrary to popular belief, the toga was normally worn only on special or formal occasions, and then usually only by the rich. It was heavy and cumbersome. For normal everyday wear tunics were worn by men and women. Trousers or leggings were considered unmanly and uncivilized. Poorer classes wore similar fashions, but made from inferior materials.

FOLLOWERS OF FASHION

Early in the period, men sported long hair and curly beards, in the Greek fashion, but by the end of the Roman era a clean-shaven, cropped look was fashionable. Although individual fashion styles changed considerably during the course of the Roman era, the basic design of clothes remained unchanged. Both men and women wore loose-fitting garments rather than being tailored to fit. Underwear was worn, but again, this was loose-fitting. Tunics were usually cut from one large piece of material, fastened at the shoulder by a brooch (as shown here) or a decorative pin.

Art & Architecture

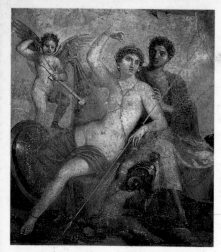

WALL PAINTINGS

Most Roman buildings, especially the villas of the wealthy and the interiors of temples, were decorated with fine wall murals, usually depicting scenes from mythology or the exploits of the gods. They were usually painted directly onto the plaster so few have survived, but those that have display a vivid realism.

*T*he Romans copied, or adapted, many Greek architectural styles, adding their own embellishments and improving the designs. They made greater use of arches than the Greeks, developing the semi-circular arch. Although massively constructed, such techniques allowed the Romans to build higher and on a grander scale than had previously been possible. By adding a volcanic material called *pozzolana* (and other minerals) to their cement they also created an incredibly strong form of concrete, stronger even than the materials it bonded together. This enabled masons to build strong walls at a much quicker rate than before, comprising an outer and inner wall of dressed stones with rubble in-fill.

The Romans built on a monumental scale and decorated the interiors of their buildings with polished marble, fine mosaics and paintings.

HEIGHTS OF PERFECTION

The Romans achieved greater heights for their buildings by erecting walls with several tiers of arches (see picture of the aqueduct on page 17). They also developed the semi-circular arch and invented the dome, enabling them to roof buildings in stone.

MOSAICS

Many Roman buildings were decorated with mosaics on the floor or walls. Mosaics are pictures made by carefully laying small, brightly painted and enamelled squared stones into wet plaster to form a picture or decorative design. They were also extremely hard-wearing and many have survived. Skilled mosaic layers called on wealthy villa owners with pattern books from which they chose a design.

FORTIFICATIONS

The Romans built massive fortifications to protect their empire, either in the form of strong city walls or forts to protect their legions. In Britain, to defend their northernmost outpost from attacks by the Scots, the Emperor Hadrian built a huge defensive wall right across the country from east to west. It was 75 miles (120 km) long, 15 feet (4.6 metres) high, and 10 feet (3 metres) thick. Much of it still survives today.

TOOLS OF THE TRADE

These tools were used by a Roman stonemason and are similar to those still in use today. On the left is a bronze square for measuring 45° and 90° angles. The dividers (right) were used to transfer measurements from scaled building plans directly onto stone. They were especially used to create intricate carvings.

EPHESUS

The Roman remains at Ephesus in western Turkey are amongst the finest to be seen anywhere. Although the Romans admired the elegant lines of Greek architecture, as their empire expanded and they took over Greek territories, they often replaced Greek buildings with their own, as at Ephesus. Many of the civic buildings survive at Ephesus, including the library of Celsius, shown here.

Health & Medicine

Although the Romans understood the importance of personal hygiene, clean water, and drainage systems to prevent disease, their knowledge of medicine was still somewhat primitive. They were a superstitious people who largely believed that diseases were a curse, given by the gods who had been in some way offended. Because of this, many people sought cures by supernatural means, by visiting healing shrines or by carrying lucky talismans to ward off evil spirits. Most physicians were Greek and they relied heavily upon herbal remedies, which were quite effective for most everyday ailments. There were no cures for more serious complaints. Surgery was basic and crudely executed, without any form of anaesthetic. Many operations were amputations or for wounds sustained in battle. Most legions had their own doctors who travelled with them to tend to the wounded, many of whom died even after treatment from secondary infections or gangrene.

ROMAN BATHS

Water supplies in the Roman world were very sophisticated and were not improved upon in Europe until the 19th century. Most towns had public water fountains, bath houses and toilets. Romans also recognized the health benefits of hot and cold plunge baths to purge and revitalize the system. These shown here are at Bath, in England.

HEALING HANDS

This detail from a wall mural shows Aeneas, a legendary war hero, having an arrow-head removed from his leg by a surgeon. Antiseptic ointments, made from herbs such as thyme, were applied in the form of a poultice. Even so, it was common for wounds to become infected or turn gangrenous, resulting in amputation, or even death, from quite minor injuries.

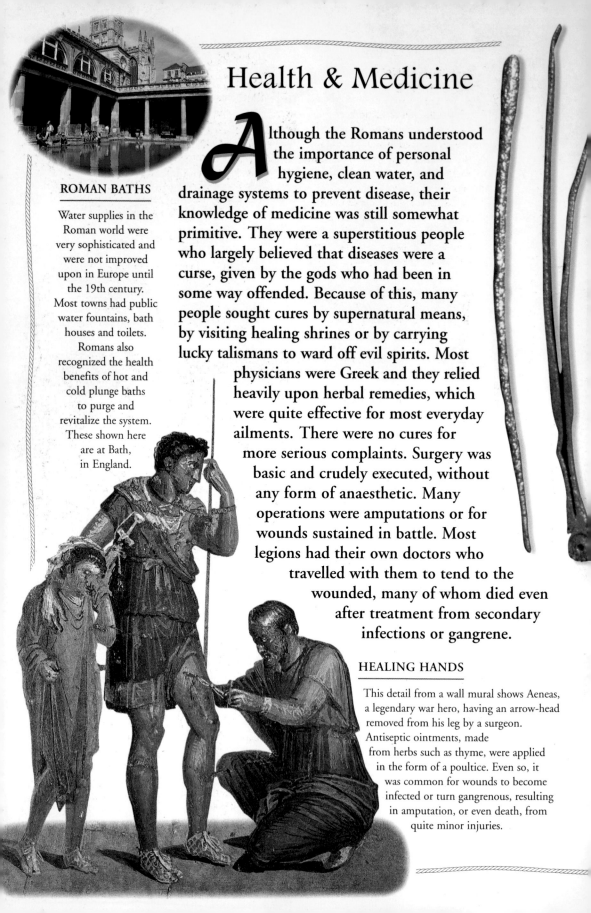

THE APPLIANCE OF SCIENCE

This collection of surgical instruments was in use throughout the Roman period and is not too dissimilar to those still used up until the 19th century. It includes knives and scalpels for making incisions, hooks to manipulate blood vessels and organs during an operation and spatulas for mixing and applying ointments or for internal examinations. Human anatomy was little understood and many patients died from shock or trauma on the operating table.

FRESH WATER

Romans developed a way to bring in fresh water supplies across deep valleys, as shown by this impressive aqueduct at Nimes, in France. Water was carried in a covered channel built into the top tier.

PERSONAL HYGIENE

This fragment of a hair comb is made of ivory and is inscribed with a relief depicting a religious ceremony. It probably belonged to a rich person, but even the poor were fastidious about their personal hygiene and used combs made of wood or bone to remove head lice.

NATURE'S CURE-ALL

The use of garlic for medicinal purposes had been widespread probably since ancient Egyptian times. It was also claimed to have the power to remove evil spirits so, to the Romans, it was doubly effective. They used it as a purgative to cleanse the system, and crushed it was an antiseptic ointment for wounds and the treatment of leprosy. Soldiers were given a daily dose to improve their general well-being.

CLEAN WATER SUPPLIES

The Romans developed a sophisticated system of water supply. Clean water was collected in huge reservoirs in the countryside, and piped into smaller feeder tanks in the towns. They also recognised the importance of keeping drinking water well away from drainage systems to prevent disease.

CUPID'S ARROW

Cupid (known to the Greeks as Eros) was the son of Venus. He was the winged god of love who carried a magical bow and arrow. If Cupid fired an arrow into the hearts of a man and a woman they were said to fall hopelessly in love with one another.

GOD OF FERTILITY

Bacchus, the Roman god of wine, was also the god of fertility (after the Greek Dionysus). He is often associated with merry-making and wedding feasts. Festivities would often degenerate into rowdiness and unrestrained merry-making, as shown in this sarcophagus frieze.

THE WEDDING CEREMONY

This figurine shows the goddess Vesta giving her blessing to a wedding ceremony. As goddess of the hearth, it was customary to make offerings to Vesta (and other gods) to ensure a happy family life after marriage. Sometimes this might take the form of an animal sacrifice. Often the wedding ceremony took place at the home of the bride's parents.

THE GODDESS OF LOVE

The Greek goddess of love and beauty was Aphrodite, whom the Romans renamed Venus. She is nearly always shown naked, or semi-clothed, and depicted as a beautiful young woman. In Roman mythology, Venus was the divine ancestor of Julius Caesar's family, which caused many to resent them because of their supposed familiarity with the gods. It was considered good luck to bless her altar on the wedding day because she was also the goddess of fertility. She possessed a magic girdle which reputedly made the wearer irresistibly attractive.

GIRL POWER

This detail from a frieze at Pompeii, in the 'Villa of Mysteries', shows a young woman's initiation into religious mysteries. Unlike men who became priests and were allowed to marry, women who entered the priesthood were expected to remain virgins and unmarried.

Love & Marriage

Many of today's marriage ceremonies and rituals are derived from the Romans. A wedding ring, for example, (usually plain to symbolise virtue) was placed on the third finger of the left hand because a nerve was thought to run from there directly to the heart. The bride wore a white toga with a coloured veil, and a feast was held at the house of the bride's father where a wedding cake was served to the guests. Marriages were usually arranged between both sets of parents and girls could be married as young as thirteen; boys were usually a little older. The girl's parents were normally expected to give a dowry of money and goods to the groom's family. Most women were considered to be the property of their husbands and regained their property only on his death. Understandably most chose not to remarry.

DUTIFUL WIVES

Women were expected to be dutiful wives and mothers. The more wealthy were allowed greater freedom, but most were expected to obey their husbands. Disobedience would normally be punished. This wall painting from the 1st century AD shows the everyday appearance of a wealthy married couple.

DEVOTED COUPLE

The Greek colony of Etruria in northern Italy was instrumental in the founding of Rome and greatly influenced Roman civilization. This magnificent Etruscan sarcophagus dating back to the 6th century BC comes from the tomb of a devoted husband and wife who share the same grave.

Women & Children

As in most other civilizations of the past, life for Roman women was hard. Women experienced a great deal of prejudice and were usually regarded as second-class citizens in Roman society. Wealth determined the amount of freedom and independence a woman might enjoy. Most were expected to keep house for the family, work in the fields and tend to such mundane jobs as spinning and weaving. Only wealthy children were educated, usually by private tutors or, more rarely, by attending school. Girls were usually only educated to a very basic standard and were then expected to learn domestic duties. Only boys were educated beyond that and groomed for a profession. Poor women were usually confined to working in the fields or becoming servants. Those slightly more well-off might secure a job in a shop, or become hairdressers. The lucky few might become a priestess (such as tending the shrine of the Vestal Virgins) but openings were few, and only for the rich.

MIDWIFERY

One of the few occupations nearing a profession that was open to women was midwifery. Giving birth was dangerous and many babies and mothers died. The Romans are thought to have first performed a Caesarean section operation when Julius Caesar was born by this method. His name is thought to have come from the Latin word *caesus*, meaning 'cut'.

WORKING ON THE LAND

The majority of country dwellers eked out a subsistence standard of living off the land. The Romans developed more efficient methods of agriculture but life was still hard, each family tending its own animals and crops. Most of the menial jobs were performed by women and children. These included sowing seeds, tending the crops, feeding the poultry, collecting the eggs, milking the cows and cheese-making.

PLAYTHINGS

Children played with a variety of toys, some of which were quite sophisticated. These pieces are from a game similar to dominoes. Boys might have played with lead soldiers and marbles, while girls had rag dolls.

THE VESTAL VIRGINS

Only rich women could become priestesses and then only for certain gods and goddesses. The cult of Vesta was particularly associated with women. Granted the gift of perpetual virginity, her shrine and holy flame in Rome was attended by a select group of priestesses known as the Vestal Virgins.

JUNO

The patron goddess of women was Juno, one of Jupiter's consorts (the other was Minerva). She is normally shown seated, as in this fine terracotta statue, usually accompanied by a peacock, her symbol. She is a very maternal figure, the protectress of women, especially during childbirth. Originally, she was the goddess of the moon, the queen of heaven.

SONG & DANCE

Isis was an Egyptian god adopted by the Romans, and is particularly associated with women and children and the cycle of life. This relief, probably from a child's sarcophagus, was found south of Rome and shows women and children dancing as part of a religious ritual to Isis.

CHILDHOOD

This child wears a *bulla* (lucky charm) around his neck, which would have been given to him at a naming ceremony conducted a few days after his birth. The inscription below includes a dedication to the spirits of the dead, which indicates that this a relief from the child's tomb. Child mortality was high with only half expected to reach age 20.

War & Weaponry

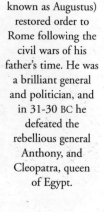

AUGUSTUS
63 BC-AD 14

Caesar's adopted son Octavian (later known as Augustus) restored order to Rome following the civil wars of his father's time. He was a brilliant general and politician, and in 31-30 BC he defeated the rebellious general Anthony, and Cleopatra, queen of Egypt.

From the 8th century BC until about 509 BC, Rome was ruled by her Etruscan neighbours in the north. When Rome became a republic in that year, the Romans removed the Etruscan king, Tarquin the Proud, from office and ruled themselves. Rome's power gradually grew to take control of much of Italy. Around 260 BC, Rome clashed with Carthage, a north-African state, so beginning a century of bitter wars. When Rome emerged victorious in 146 BC it had acquired its first overseas dominions. In order to gain victory, Rome had to organize a highly disciplined army, which then went on to conquer neighbouring lands. By AD 50 most of the Mediterranean basin had fallen to the might of the Roman legions.

GALLEYS

Roman warships, known as galleys, were propelled by a combination of sail and oar, with slaves as oarsmen. They had a huge battering ram on the bow to ram enemy ships. Although siege engines were sometimes mounted on deck, Roman ships were mostly used to transport troops or act as mere fighting platforms.

HANNIBAL

Rome's second attempt to invade Carthage was thwarted by Hannibal, a brilliant general who marched his army with forty war elephants across northern Africa, Spain, and across the Alps to Italy, to launch a surprise attack on Rome itself. Initially, Hannibal enjoyed some success but was eventually beaten in 202 BC.

PRIDE OF ROME

Roman legions consisted of about 5,000 infantrymen and were the pride of the Empire's army. They were supplemented by auxiliary cavalry who covered their flanks in an attack and scouted ahead, and by ordinary foot-soldiers, whose job it was to man the frontier forts protecting the Empire from attack or rebellion. In command of each legion was a centurion who wore a distinctive helmet, such as this one, complete with crests or plumes, so he could be easily seen and followed in battle. Legionnaires were well-equipped and highly trained. They are believed to be the first army in history to be paid regular wages as a proper occupation.

LEGIONNAIRES

It is generally accepted that the success of the Roman Empire lay with its highly disciplined fighting legions. Earlier civilisations, including the Greeks and the Etruscans before them, proved incapable of raising and maintaining a centrally organised army. This severely limited their ability at sustained or widespread conquest. Without a standing army new colonies soon collapsed. By contrast, wherever the Romans conquered they left behind a strong military presence to consolidate their gains.

JULIUS CAESAR

Civil war frequently broke out in the 'old' republic of Rome as generals competed for power. Julius Caesar (*c.*100-44 BC) declared himself supreme dictator, but he was assassinated by his fellow senators who found he had become too powerful.

ROMAN WEAPONS

Roman weapons were usually made of iron or steel, with wooden or bone hand grips. Legionnaires were usually armed with a dagger and a sword. They favoured short-bladed swords with double-edged blades, used as a stabbing weapon. Foot soldiers also used throwing spears, short bows and javelins, hurling them en masse into their enemy's midst.

SIEGE ENGINES

The most common form of Roman siege weapon was the *ballista*, as shown here. This impressive piece of military equipment could hurl a large boulder several hundred metres. They were also used to throw faggots of burning sticks and straw amongst enemy ships.

Crime & Punishment

The centre of Roman lawmaking was the Senate in Rome itself, where members, known as senators, were voted into office and decisions of government arrived at after lengthy discussion. The system was open to abuse, however, and laws tended to be made, or repealed, more to appease public popularity than necessarily to be fair. The Romans first introduced the idea of magistrates' courts where crimes and grievances were heard. Punishment very often took the form of compensation rather than retribution and there were few prisons. Criminals sometimes had their sentences commuted to slavery, even if they were Roman citizens. Even offences against one of the many gods might have been considered a crime. Each city had an elected council of about 100 men, who usually held office for life.

THE NEW REPUBLIC

Following the chaos of civil war, which had led to the assassination of Julius Caesar, it fell upon his adopted son, Augustus, to restore order. Fortunately, he proved to be an able politician who carried out many reforms. He declared Rome a 'new' republic and himself its first emperor.

CRUCIFIXION

Crucifixion was a common form of execution in Roman times and was not, as many suppose, reserved for religious victims. Death was slow and excruciatingly painful. Usually the victim's arms were tied above his head onto a single pole, sometimes they were fastened to a cross with their arms outstretched. Either way, the lungs gradually collapsed, causing death by asphyxiation.

CORRUPTION

The Romans took pride in having one of the fairest and most democratic constitutions of any nation in the known world. However, the system was open to abuse. Laws tended to be made, or repealed, more for public popularity than to be fair. The Senate was frequently the subject of corruption charges, leading to military unrest and civil war as powerful generals tried to seize control. As the power of Rome began to fade and economic chaos set in, many senators fell victim to bribery by rich merchants.

TRIAL BY COMBAT

Many of those who were called upon to do battle in the Colosseum (as shown above) were criminals or religious martyrs. It amused the people to see such victims compete against wild animals or ruthless gladiators in an effort to gain their freedom. Even if they survived, many were trained to become gladiators themselves, living under the constant threat of death in the arena.

THE PRICE OF HOMAGE

The relief on this coin shows Augustus receiving a child from a barbarian. It was customary for emperors, following a great victory, to be presented with captured offspring in homage. Many conquered people became slaves; any who refused to pay homage were executed. Captured leaders were often executed by strangulatio to serve as an example to newly conquered people.

DEATH BY EXECUTION

The Romans ruled their empire by might and oppression. Many crimes carried the death sentence, including stealing and treason. The methods of execution were equally varied. This illustration shows some of them; death by sword, axe and stoning.

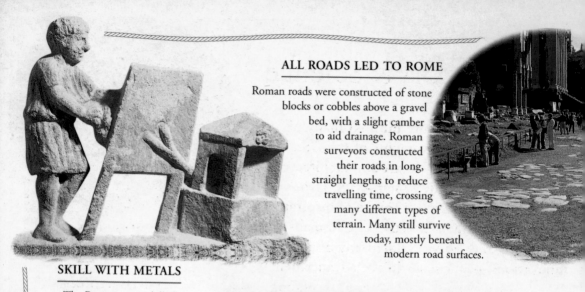

ALL ROADS LED TO ROME

Roman roads were constructed of stone blocks or cobbles above a gravel bed, with a slight camber to aid drainage. Roman surveyors constructed their roads in long, straight lengths to reduce travelling time, crossing many different types of terrain. Many still survive today, mostly beneath modern road surfaces.

SKILL WITH METALS

The Romans were skilled metalworkers, making tools, weapons, utensils and intricate jewellery. They could not perfect the technique of smelting iron, so they heated solid pieces and hammered it into shape (forging). They made several alloys, including bronze (copper and tin) to which they added zinc to resemble gold.

MAN POWER

Sailing in Roman times was still a dangerous enterprise and usually undertaken only in good weather. Navigation was crude and relied on simple observation and plotting movements of the moon, stars and planets. The cargo ship shown in this mosaic would have been wind-powered (the mast is lowered), but supplementary power would have been provided by slave oarsmen for extra propulsion in calm weather.

LIGHTHOUSES

The ruin of this Roman pharos (lighthouse) can still be seen on the cliffs at Dover Castle, Kent. Originally, an identical structure stood on the opposite cliff. Lights were kept burning in the top tiers to guide ships into harbour.

ROAD TRANSPORT

Merchants used either pack animals or carts, pulled by oxen or horses, to transport their goods to market. Chariots, small two-wheeled carts pulled by up to four horses harnessed abreast, were only used for warfare and later specially adapted for racing.

Transport & Science

The Romans admired many of the achievements of the Greeks, particularly in art and architecture, and often emulated their styles. However, they used Greece more as a source of inspiration rather than copying them directly. The Romans went on to introduce and develop many of their own innovations, particularly in the advancement of technology. They recognized the importance of a clean water supply to good health and so perfected a system of piping and drainage in their towns and villas. This lead to the development of plunge baths, and the invention of the hypocaust, their ingenious under-floor central heating system. In architecture they invented a new form of very strong concrete and improved the way bricks were manufactured. The Romans' use of arches allowed them to span greater distances than previous civilizations had been able to achieve and led to the invention of the dome. In glassmaking, they developed the new technique of glass-blowing, which made more intricate shapes possible. But perhaps the greatest success of the Roman Empire was the network of roads they constructed to facilitate rapid movement of soldiers and supplies.

ALL MOD CONS

This view shows the ruins of the Roman baths at Carthage, built between AD 145-162. It clearly shows the hypocaust, where the floor was raised on pillars to allow the passage of hot air from adjoining furnaces. Grills in the floor above allowed the hot air to rise and heat the rooms.

CENTRAL HEATING

The hypocaust was a system of central heating based upon the principle that hot air rises. It both heated the water and warmed the rooms of private houses and public baths. This view shows how the system worked. Hypocausts were particularly popular in houses in the north, where it was colder in the winter.

Religion

Many of the gods in the Roman world were borrowed from ancient Greek mythology. The Romans renamed them, but also had a very different attitude towards them. Whereas the Greeks gave their gods a human familiarity, the Romans were a far more superstitious people, who went in fear of their gods and made votive offerings to ward off evil spirits. They were also not averse to accumulating the gods and religious beliefs of the peoples they conquered, adding them to their own rich montage of beliefs. Romans posted to the outlying regions of the Empire, such as Celtic Britain, frequently adopted their customs. Gradually, some Romans began to embrace Christianity, frequently worshipping the Christian God alongside their own. By about AD 337 Christianity had become the main religion of the Roman Empire.

PIVS SEXTVS P·M·REST·

APOLLO

Unlike all the other gods, Apollo was known by the same name to both the Greeks and Romans. He was the god of the sun and considered the most benevolent of all gods.

MITHRAISM

Mithras was originally the Persian god of light, identified with the sun. Here we see him slaying a bull in ritual sacrifice, to fertilize the world with its blood. Many soldiers in the Roman army adopted Mithraism as their religion.

GOD OF WAR

Mars was the Roman god of war and is usually depicted as a powerful soldier clad in full armour. The month of March is named in honour of him. He was the second most powerful god, after Jupiter. He is also associated with agriculture and many of his festivals were linked to the rural calendar, particularly spring and autumn.

KINGS OF THE GODS

The most powerful of all the Roman gods was Jupiter, who was said to have resided on the Capitol Hill in Rome itself, overseeing the honour of the Empire. He was the god of light and the sky, symbolized by thunder and the eagle.

FEMALE CULTS

A few Roman religions were associated almost exclusively with women and fertility, such as Cybele, Isis and Vesta. This view shows the temple of Vesta, in Rome.

CATACOMBS

Although early Roman Christians may have used catacombs as a secret meeting place, their original purpose was as a place of burial, the bodies being placed in niches in the walls. The rock-hewn tunnel in this view leads to the shrine of the Sybil at Cumae. The Sybil was a devotee of Apollo, endowed by him with the gift of prophecy.

GODDESS OF WISDOM

The Roman goddess Minerva equates to the Greek Athena and was the goddess of handicrafts and wisdom. She is often depicted, as here, in a warlike stance to symbolize the power of the Empize and adopted by the army to decorate their shields and armour. Britannia, who came to represent Britain, is thought to be based on her.

SACRIFICES

Sacrificial altars, although considered essential to many Roman religions, were generally placed outside the entrances to temples. A statue of the relevant god was placed inside.

Legacy of the Past

When studying the remains of Roman society today it is easy to get a false impression of what life was like. Almost all of the remains are of the impressive stone buildings, especially civic buildings, temples and villas, because these have better endured the passage of time. Although Roman society as a whole was rich and technologically brilliant, only the elite few enjoyed a luxurious lifestyle and we should temper our impression of their civilization by trying to imagine what life might have been like for ordinary people. However, there is no doubt that the Roman Empire left a legacy which has lasted right up to the present day. Many European roads are built over old Roman roads. Modern plumbing and sewerage systems owe much to the Romans; as does Western architecture and language. Other facets of their society, such as literature, military strategy and law, still influence us today.

ROAD BUILDING

Perhaps the greatest legacy left behind by the Romans was their engineering skills, particularly in road making. Many roads were not vastly improved until the 19th century and often follow their original Roman course.

CLASSIC DESIGNS

Few Roman buildings survive anywhere in their entirety, but they have served as a source of inspiration to builders down the ages. In the 11th and 12th centuries, Norman architects emulated their style (now known as Romanesque) and in 18th- and 19th-century Britain architects borrowed many classical designs for their buildings.

THE EMPIRE DIVIDES

In AD 395, the Roman Empire was divided into two states, east and west. By 476, the Western Empire had fallen to invaders from the north and become fully Christianized. The Eastern Empire remained virtually intact for another 1,000 years, calling itself Byzantium. Many of the Roman traditions prevailed including architectural styles, as this mausoleum shows.

THE FALL
OF THE EMPIRE

In AD 406, Germanic tribes overran
the Rhine border in the north and
in 410, Rome itself was sacked.
The army was called back to
defend Rome from the furthest
outposts, including Britain. By 476
the Western Empire had fallen.

ATTILA THE HUN (C.AD 406-53)

The Roman Empire reached its zenith around AD 200,
after which time it began to break up. There was continuous civil
war at home and the Empire was under constant attack along its
many borders, particularly from the Persians in the east, and
the Germanic tribes of the north. Chief among these were
the Huns from central Asia. Attila the Hun was a ruthless
warrior, known as the 'scourge of god'. He extended
his territory from the Rhine to China and in AD 447
defeated the Roman emperor Theodosius.

THE STATES OF
MODERN EUROPE

The break up of the
Roman Empire
was largely
responsible for
the formation of
modern Europe.
In the north, Franks
settled in what is now
France and the Saxons invaded
England. In the east, Turkey retained
elements of both east and west, as it still does.
This view shows St Sophia Mosque in Istanbul.

UNIQUE SURVIVAL

The excavated city of Pompeii is a unique record of the
Roman world. In AD 79 the city, located near present-
day Naples, was destroyed (along with the neighbouring
town of Herculaneum) when the volcano Vesuvius
suddenly erupted. For 1700 years the city and its
people lay buried beneath the ash. Modern excavations
have revealed a city virtually untouched by time, showing
all aspects of everyday life for rich and poor alike.

DID YOU KNOW?

That the Romans used asbestos shrouds?
The Romans knew of the fireproof properties of asbestos and wrapped corpses in an asbestos shroud before being cremated. In this way, although the body burned within the funeral pyre, the ashes could be kept separate from the rest of the fire and placed in urns, pure and undefiled. The Vestal Virgins are also believed to have used asbestos lamp wicks to ensure that the flame at the shrine of Vesta never burnt out.

That pantomime may have its origins in ancient Rome? Every year, just after Christmas, pantomimes are conducted in theatres throughout Europe, where chaos and mayhem are the order of the day. Pantomimes may have their origins in the Roman festival of Kalends, where the everyday world was temporarily turned upside down. Revellers dressed in animal masks and engaged in off-key singing during mock church services. Men and women changed roles and satirical verses were recited. The festival was known as the 'Feast of Fools'.

That Rome first introduced passports?
To ensure the safe passage of merchants and political envoys within the Empire and through foreign lands, the Romans issued a 'certificate of safe conduct' which was shown to the ruler of each country passed through on a journey. The certificate carried the full protection of Rome and contained words of warning to any foreign official who did not honour it and allow the safe passage of its bearer.

That Romans cut the largest stone blocks in the world? At Baalbek, in Lebanon, stand the ruins of a group of Roman temples surrounded by a massive stone wall. The three largest stones are known as the trilithon. Cut from a quarry about a mile away, transported and lifted into position about 8 metres (25 ft) high, the biggest stone measures 21 metres (67 ft) long, by about 4 metres (13 ft) square and weighs an incredible 800 tonnes. The stones were laid so precisely that the joints are almost an exact fit. How, and why, the stones were put in position remains a mystery.

That the excavated remains of Pompeii are like a window into the past? When Mount Vesuvius erupted in AD 79 the molten lava and hot ash spread so quickly that over 2,000 of the city's population of 20,000 were unable to escape. The bodies of people fleeing the choking fumes have been discovered in the streets, encased in solidified lava. Some people were killed in mid-action, such as a customer being served with a drink in a wine bar and a baker who had just put some loaves into an oven. The remains at Pompeii are still in the process of careful excavation to reveal the everyday lives of ordinary people, frozen in time.

ACKNOWLEDGEMENTS

We would like to thank: Graham Rich and Elizabeth Wiggans for their assistance and David Hobbs for his map of the world.

Copyright © 1998 ticktock Publishing Ltd.

First published in Great Britain by ticktock Publishing Ltd., The Offices in the Square, Hadlow, Tonbridge, Kent, TN11 0DD. All rights reserved.

No part of this publication may be reproduced, stored in a retrieval system, or transmitted in any form or by any means electronic, mechanical, photocopying, recording or otherwise, without prior written permission of the copyright owner.

A CIP catalogue record for this book is available from the British Library. ISBN 1 86007 072 8

Picture research by Image Select. Printed in Hong Kong.

Picture Credits:
t=top, b=bottom, c=centre, l=left, r=right, OFC=outside front cover, IFC=inside front cover, IBC=inside back cover, OBC=outside back cover

AKG; London 10/11, 17br, 23ct, 24bl. Alinari - Giraudon, Paris; 7tl, 9cb, 14bl, 19tr, 31br. Ancient Art and Architecture; 18cl, 23cb, 22/23ct. Ann Ronan at Image Select; 7cr, 7cb, 17tr, 17bl, 22cb, 23r, 23b, 24tl, 26br, 26/27c, 26tr, 28l, 29br, 31tr & OBC. Archives Larousse - Giraudon; 10/11cb & OFC. Bridgeman Art Library; 16/17ct, 17cr, 27br. Chris Fairclough Colour Library / Image Select; 6cr, 15r, 16tl, 20bl, 30/31c. Corbis Bettman; OFC (main pic). et Archive; 24br. Gilles Mermet - Giraudon; 18/19ct, 22bl. Giraudon; 2/3cb, 2tl, 4c, 6b, 6tl, 8bl, 8cr, 10r & OFC, 12/13cb, 12tl, 14tl, 15tl, 16bl, 19b, 21tr, 21tl, 25b, 25t & IFC, 26tl, 26bl, 26/27c, 28c, 28b, 29tr, 30b. Image Select International; 2/3ct & OBC, 3br, 3tr, 5tr, 5cb, 9tl, 10tr & OFC, 10tl, 13br, 12/13ct, 12bl, 15br, 14/15b, 22tl, 29tl & OBC, 29c, 30/31c. Pix; 30tl. Spectrum Colour Library; 8tl. The Telegraph Colour Library; 30l. Werner Forman Archive; 5cr, 4tr, 4b, 4tl, 9r & OFC, 11tr, 13tr, 18tl & OBC, 18bl, 18c, 20tl, 20br, 21b, 25c, 27tr, 29cb.

Every effort has been made to trace the copyright holders and we apologize in advance for any unintentional omissions.
We would be pleased to insert the appropriate acknowledgement in any subsequent edition of this publication.

snapping-turtle
guide